P9-CQE-955

WHAT HAPPENED TO THE
DINOSAURS?

by Franklyn M. Branley
illustrated by Marc Simont

HARPERCOLLINSPUBLISHERS

Special thanks to Armand Morgan, of the
Peabody Museum of Natural History,
for his time and expert review.

The *Let's-Read-and-Find-Out Science* book series was originated by Dr. Franklyn M. Branley, Astronomer Emeritus and former Chairman of the American Museum–Hayden Planetarium, and was formerly co-edited by him and Dr. Roma Gans, Professor Emeritus of Childhood Education, Teachers College, Columbia University. Text and illustrations for each of the books in the series are checked for accuracy by an expert in the relevant field. For more information about Let's-Read-and-Find-Out Science books, write to HarperCollins Children's Books, 1350 Avenue of the Americas, New York, NY 10019, or visit our web site at www.harperchildrens.com.

HarperCollins®, ♣®, and Let's Read-and-Find-Out Science® are trademarks of HarperCollins Publishers Inc.

WHAT HAPPENED TO THE DINOSAURS?
Text copyright © 1989 by Franklyn M. Branley
Illustrations copyright © 1989 by Marc Simont
All rights reserved. Printed in the U.S.A.

Library of Congress Cataloging-in-Publication Data
Branley, Franklyn Mansfield, 1915–
   What happened to the dinosaurs?
(Let's-read-and-find-out science. Stage 2)
   Summary: Describes various scientific theories which explore the extinction of the dinosaurs.
   ISBN 0-690-04747-9. — ISBN 0-690-04749-5 (lib. bdg.). — ISBN 0-06-445105-4 (pbk.)
   1. Dinosaurs—Juvenile literature.   2. Extinction (Biology)—Juvenile literature.   [1. Dinosaurs.   2. Extinction (Biology).]
I. Simont, Marc, ill.   II. Title.   III. Series.
QE862.D5B66   1989   88-37626
597.9'1

WHAT HAPPENED TO THE
DINOSAURS?

What happened to the dinosaurs?

Dinosaurs lived on Earth for 160 million years. Then, 65 million years ago, most of them disappeared. A few smaller ones slowly changed into the birds we have today.

Other reptiles disappeared, too—flying reptiles and reptiles that lived in the sea. Many other kinds of animals also died out. And many kinds of plants.

No one knows why the dinosaurs disappeared. But there are many different ideas. Scientists look at the evidence and try to decide which idea is right.

Maybe small animals ate dinosaur eggs so only a few eggs were able to hatch. This is one idea. But it does not explain why other kinds of animals died out, and many plants as well. Also, some dinosaurs may not have laid eggs.

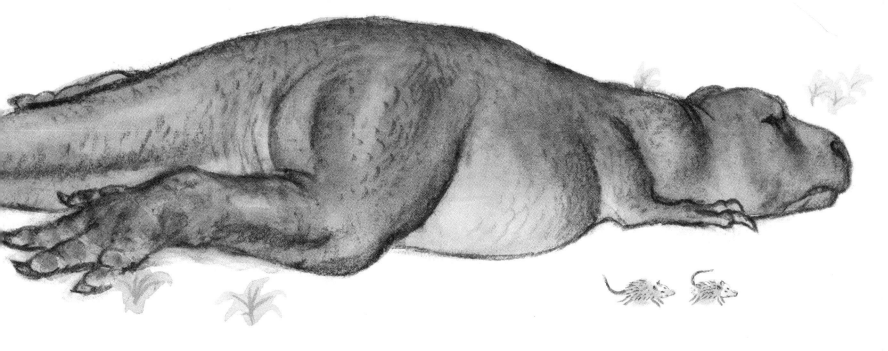

Maybe a group of dinosaurs got sick and the sickness spread to other groups. That's possible, for even today diseases spread among herds of cattle. But if that happened, chances are the sickness would not have reached reptiles that lived in the sea. Also, other kinds of animals would not have caught the sickness, and neither would plants.

Some scientists have another idea. They study fossils in very old layers of rock and in newer layers, too. They think they see signs that every 26 to 30 million years, different kinds of animals and plants have died out.

Maybe every 26 to 30 million years showers of comets hit Earth. These comet showers would change Earth so much that many living things would not survive.

14

But, they wonder, why should the comet showers occur every 26 to 30 million years? Why should they happen so regularly? Some people answer the question this way: They say that the sun has a twin. The two stars move around one another, and it takes about 26 million years for them to go around once. No one has found such a star, but it has been named. It is called the Nemesis star. ("Nemesis" means "trouble." When the dinosaurs met their nemesis, they were in trouble.)

16

Way out beyond the solar system, we know, there is a huge cloud of dust. Comets come from this cloud.

Maybe every 26 million years the Nemesis star comes in closer to the cloud and pulls dust out of it. The dust collects together, making clusters of comets. The comets race through space, most of them becoming space wanderers. But many collide with our planet. If this idea is correct, there will be comet collisions in the future. The next one would be about 13 million years from now.

Another idea was suggested by scientists who were exploring old layers of rocks. In rock layers 65 million years old they found dinosaur fossils. They also found iridium. That's a rare metal, most of which is deep inside the earth. Another scientist found a layer of black soot, or carbon, that might have been produced by a great fire.

Traces of iridium have been found in meteorites that have fallen to Earth. And scientists believe that the metal may be found in asteroids, too. Asteroids are planetlike masses in orbit between Mars and Jupiter. Occasionally asteroids escape that orbit and collide with Earth.

Sixty-five million years ago a huge asteroid may have crashed into Earth. That would have produced a lot of heat. Wildfires would have swept through forests and swamps. Only small animals that could dig into the ground would have escaped.

21

After the fire had burned out, some people say, the air was heavy with soot, ash, and dust. There was so much, the sun could not shine through. Earth got colder and colder. Many plants that had survived the fire could not grow.

Dinosaurs that ate plants could not find enough to eat. So they starved. Meat-eating dinosaurs who ate the plant eaters would have starved, too.

The dust cloud may have hung over Earth for many months or even a year. Gradually it settled, making the layers of iridium and soot that scientists have discovered.

The idea is very possible, for we know there have been other collisions with Earth. For example, in 1908 something crashed into Siberia, a part of Russia. It flattened trees and caused flash fires. The object may have been an asteroid, or several of them.

We know *what* happened to the dinosaurs. They disappeared.
But we do not know why. We think there are many ways it could
have happened.

Maybe the correct answer is in one of these different ideas. Many people strongly believe there was a tremendous asteroid collision, and wild Earth fire. Dust and ash may have darkened the skies and blocked out the sun. Maybe there is a Nemesis star that passes near the dust cloud every 26 million years.

No one knows. But we can be sure that scientists will keep trying to find out which idea is the right one.

Why the dinosaurs disappeared is still a mystery.